Contents

Nuclear power? No thanks?

At the beginning of the 20th century, science was just beginning to discover **radioactivity**. It was also taking its first steps towards discovering how **atoms** are put together. (Atoms are the particles from which all matter is made.) In 1905 the German scientist Albert Einstein, in his 'theory of relativity', showed that **mass** could be changed into energy. In 1918 Sir Ernest Rutherford had shown that atoms could be split. By 1942 the world had its first nuclear **reactor**.

Anti-nuclear protestors demonstrated for a month against the Superphénix reactor in France.

By the 1990s nuclear power was the second biggest source of energy, after **fossil fuels**, for the industrialized world. For many people **nuclear energy** was the answer to the problem of shrinking oil and coal resources and to the pollution that burning these fossil fuels causes. However, today the nuclear industry has stopped growing.

Reactor reactions

Many people are worried about the **environmental** and health aspects of nuclear power. Nuclear reactors produce **radiation**, which is harmful to living things. High doses of radiation can kill very quickly. Small doses (such as might leak from a normally operating nuclear plant) could build up over many years and also cause damage. But radiation is a fact of life. It comes from the Sun, from rocks, from medical X-rays, and even from televisions. Some scientists say that the average person gets five times more radiation during a lifetime of sitting in front of a television or computer than they would if they lived near a nuclear power station.

The risk of accidents at nuclear power stations is more serious. If there is a fire or explosion **radioactive** materials could escape inside the power station or even into the outside environment as well. Nuclear power is also disliked by many because of its connection with nuclear weapons.

Reactor number one at Calder Hall, Cumberland – Britain's first nuclear power station – opened in October 1956.

Inside the atom

To understand how nuclear power works, we first have to look at the way **atoms** are put together. Atoms are the tiny particles from which you and everything around you is made. A substance made of only one type of atom is called an **element**.

An atom can be divided into two parts. There is an outer cloud of tiny particles called **electrons**. The number of electrons is important. It tells us how the atom will react with other atoms in chemical reactions.

The inner part of the atom is the **nucleus**. This is a tightly packed cluster of particles called **protons** and **neutrons**. Each element has a different number of protons and neutrons. Elements range from hydrogen, the simplest element, with a single proton, to uranium which can have 235 or more protons and neutrons. The atoms of a particular element all have the same number of protons in their nuclei.

The nucleus of an atom is made up of protons and neutrons and surrounded by orbiting electrons.

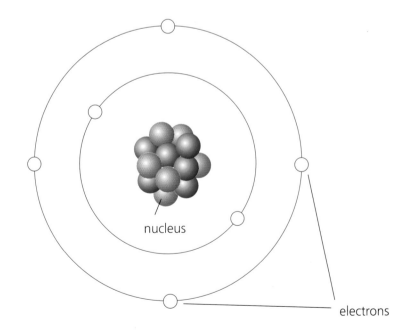

nucleus

electrons

Isotopes

It is possible for atoms of the same element to have the same number of protons, but to have different numbers of neutrons. Such atoms are called **isotopes** of that element. Isotopes may be stable (unchanging) or **radioactive**, naturally occurring, or made in a laboratory.

Radioactive elements

Of the known elements, 92 are known to occur in nature. These elements have **atomic numbers** ranging from 1 (hydrogen) to 92 (uranium). Eighty-one of these elements are stable but all the others are radioactive.

In a radioactive substance the nuclei of its atoms are unstable. They break apart, or **decay**, giving out energy as they do so. When the nucleus decays, it forms a nucleus that is more stable than it was before. The new nucleus may have fewer protons than at first, which means that it has become a different element. A radioactive element may go through several stages of decay before finally becoming a stable element.

Half-life

We cannot predict when any one radioactive nucleus will decay. However, we can say when half of the atoms in a particular sample of a radioactive material will have decayed. This is called the radioactive element's **half-life**. The half-life of uranium 238 (an isotope of uranium) is about the same as the age of the Earth, 4.5 billion years. But the half-life of polonium 213 is only a little over four millionths of a second!

Energy from the atom

Chemical reactions release energy in the form of heat. The **atoms** in a chemical reaction remain unchanged. For example, when burning coal in a fossil fuel power station, the burning atoms of carbon (in the coal) combine with atoms of oxygen (in the air) to form carbon dioxide. The atoms in a nuclear reaction do not stay the same – they change. An unstable atomic **nucleus** breaks up. As it does so, it releases energy in the form of **radioactivity**.

Missing mass

If you could weigh all the atoms present before and after a chemical reaction you would find that the weight was just the same. **Mass** is never lost in a chemical reaction. However, in a nuclear reaction mass is lost. If you add up the mass of all the particles (and the new atomic nuclei) formed by the **decay** of an unstable nucleus, you will find that it is less than the mass of the original nucleus.

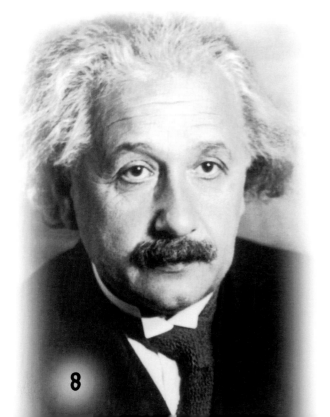

Mass and energy

At the beginning of the 20th century, Albert Einstein showed that mass and energy are linked. If mass is lost in a nuclear reaction then its equivalent in energy is released. In fact, the amount of energy released is massive. The Sun, for example, converts four million tonnes of mass into energy every second!

Albert Einstein (1879–1955) revealed the connection between matter and energy.

The energy released in a nuclear reaction amounts to 50 million times more energy per atom than can be obtained by burning an atom of carbon. Most of the energy is in the form of **kinetic energy** as the nucleus flies apart. This kinetic energy is rapidly converted into **heat energy** as the fragments of the nucleus collide with other atoms. It is this heat that is used to generate electricity in a nuclear power station. Some of the energy left over is carried off in the form of radioactivity.

Radioactive decay

When the nucleus of a **radioactive element** breaks down it can give off different types of radioactivity:

- **alpha particles** are made up of **protons** and **neutrons**. These particles are quite easy to stop

- **beta particles** are fast moving **electrons**. These particles are quite easy to stop.

- **gamma rays** are not particles at all, they are a form of **radiation** containing a lot of energy. They are not easy to stop – a thick sheet of lead is needed to block gamma rays.

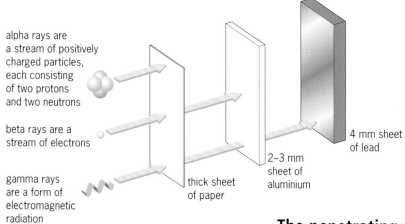

alpha rays are a stream of positively charged particles, each consisting of two protons and two neutrons

beta rays are a stream of electrons

gamma rays are a form of electromagnetic radiation

thick sheet of paper

2–3 mm sheet of aluminium

4 mm sheet of lead

The penetrating power of radioactivity.

Neutrons and chain reactions

Naturally occurring uranium contains two **isotopes**: Uranium 238 (U238) and Uranium 235 (U235). U238 is by far the most abundant, making up 99.28 per cent. U235 makes up the other 0.72 per cent. If a U235 **nucleus** is struck by a **neutron** it will **fission** (break apart). Materials that will do this are called **fissile** materials. U235 is fissile but U238 is not. As the U235 nucleus breaks apart it releases energy and two or three more neutrons.

The fission of a uranium atom.

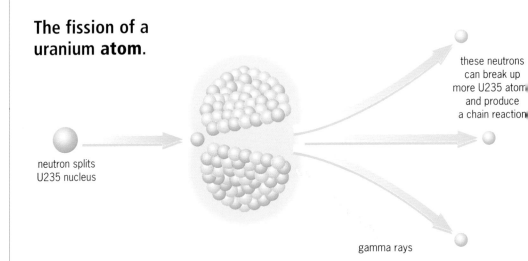

neutron splits U235 nucleus

these neutrons can break up more U235 atoms and produce a chain reaction

gamma rays

Chain reactions

The neutrons released by the fissioning uranium may strike other nuclei. If they strike U235 nuclei these will fission too, releasing still more neutrons. These neutrons can go on to strike yet more nuclei, which will release yet more neutrons, and so a **chain reaction** is set off. Within a typical nuclear power station there may be a hundred million million million fission chain reactions taking place at any time.

When a U235 atom **decays** it becomes an atom of the **element** xenon and an atom of the element strontium. These new atoms are themselves unstable and will decay further.

The chain reactions can be controlled by **control rods** made of materials that will absorb neutrons. The fewer neutrons there are flying around, the fewer fissions there will be. Nuclear power stations use **control rods** to control their power output.

Critical mass

The smallest amount of a fissile material, such as U235, that can keep a continuous chain reaction going is called the critical mass. If the amount of fissile material is much above the critical mass, the reaction may speed up and run out of control. This is called a 'supercritical' system and it is what happens in a nuclear explosion.

The power of the atom is unleashed in the first atomic bomb.

Unlocking the atom

In the early part of the 20th century a number of researchers around the world were investigating what happens when **neutrons** strike uranium **atoms**. In 1938 German scientists Otto Hahn and Fritz Strassmann showed that when uranium is bombarded with neutrons new, lighter **elements** are formed. A year later Lise Meitner and Otto Frisch came up with the term **fission** to describe this process. They said that when the uranium was struck by neutrons, it fissioned (split) into lighter elements.

Weapons of war

When World War II began governments wanted to find a way of using fission as a source of energy, especially for weapons. The United States government poured a huge amount of money and resources into what was named the Manhattan Project. The aim was to make the first atomic bomb. A team lead by Enrico Fermi made the first nuclear **reactor** at the University of Chicago on 2 December 1942. The reactor used natural uranium as its fuel.

The world's second nuclear reactor built at the Argonne Forest laboratory, Chicago, in 1943.

To make a bomb, much higher concentrations of the U235 **isotope** of uranium than occurs naturally are necessary. Part of the Manhattan Project's task was to develop a way of separating U235 from U238.

Another way to develop weapons is to use a different **fissile** material. For example, an isotope of the artificial element plutonium, Pu239, is formed in nuclear reactors and can be used to make weapons. Once Fermi had shown that a reactor could be built, people wanted reactors that could produce plutonium. The first such reactor was built in Oak Ridge, Tennessee, USA. It took less than three years to develop this entirely new technology. It also prepared the way for the development of **nuclear energy** for commercial use.

US President Eisenhower supported the use of nuclear power for peaceful, domestic uses such as the production of electricity.

'Atoms for Peace'

The Atomic Energy Commission (AEC) was set up in 1946 to oversee civilian uses of nuclear power in the United States. In December 1953, in a speech at the United Nations, US President Eisenhower announced his decision to make nuclear-related information available to other countries in order to promote the peaceful use of nuclear energy. He called this 'atoms for peace'. Britain began to produce nuclear-fuelled electricity in 1956 and the French began to build their first commercial plants in 1957. By the early 1960s nuclear power was established as an energy source across the world.

Uranium mining

Uranium is one of the less common **elements**, although it is about 20 times more common than a precious metal like silver. Uranium is usually found as uraninite, an **oxide** of uranium, also called pitchblende.

After it has been extracted the uranium is separated by crushing the rock and then treating it with chemicals. The uranium leaves the mine as yellowcake, or uranium concentrate, another oxide of uranium. A great deal of waste is produced when uranium is extracted from uraninite. Even a high-concentration **ore** will still contain only about 1 per cent uranium. For every tonne of ore processed 990 kilograms is waste.

How much uranium?

Like **fossil fuels**, uranium is nonrenewable resource. There is only a limited amount available and it is likely that all of it will be used up in fifty years or so –just when we start to run short of natural gas and petroleum. So, in the long-term uranium is not the answer to all our energy problems.

A uranium mine in Australia.

The risks of mining

Uranium is **radioactive** – and **radioactivity** can be a health hazard for people exposed to it. The radioactive waste products left behind after the uranium has been extracted are are covered with earth or returned underground to reduce the risk of **radiation** exposure.

One of these wastes is a radioactive **isotope** of the gas radon. If breathed-in it can damage the lungs. Radon tends to accumulate in underground uranium mines. Miners used to call the lung diseases they developed from breathing the radioactive dust 'mountain sickness'.

Cutting the risks, raising the costs

The average dose of radiation received by miners increases their risk of developing lung cancer by six times. The Union of Concerned Scientists in the United States says that radon levels can be reduced simply by ventilating the mines. The cost of bringing exposure down to reasonably safe levels would be between 10 and 20 per cent of the value of the uranium mined.

This is just one of the issues raised by nuclear power. If power stations buy their uranium from the cheapest source they are discouraging mines from increasing safety for the miners.

Increasing safety raises the cost of the uranium. The choice for workers in uranium mines is often between risky work or no work at all.

A sample 'button' of U235, the fuel for nuclear reactors.

Nuclear fuel production

Yellowcake is used to produce nuclear fuel. It is a raw material that has to be mined. It is purified to make uranium trioxide, and then heated to produce uranium dioxide. Naturally occurring uranium does not have a high enough proportion of U235 to sustain a nuclear **chain reaction**. Most nuclear **reactors** need to use uranium enriched with the U235 **isotope**.

Enriching uranium
There are two ways of enriching uranium. Both methods begin with processing the uranium dioxide to get uranium hexafluoride.

Gas diffusion
Lighter **molecules** of a gas will move through (**diffuse**) a porous material faster than heavier molecules. This means that molecules of uranium hexafluoride that contain U235 **atoms** will diffuse faster than molecules containing the slightly heavier U238 atoms. This process has to be repeated many times before the uranium becomes enriched enough. It also requires a great deal of energy.

Fuel production hazards
The biggest hazards of nuclear fuel production come not from possible exposure to **radiation** but from the chemicals used in the fuel processing. Fluorine and hydrogen fluoride are extremely dangerous chemicals – in fact fluorine is the most reactive of chemicals. Both can cause severe burns if they touch unprotected skin.

A gas diffusion nuclear fuel enrichment
plant in Kentucky, USA.

Gas centrifuge enrichment
Gas centrifuge enrichment plants are smaller and less
expensive to operate than gas diffusion plants. In this
method the uranium hexafluoride is spun in a cylinder
at around 1000 revolutions per second. The heavier
U238-containing molecules tend to move towards the
wall of the container more easily, leaving the lighter
U235 molecules in the centre. This separation is far
from perfect, but gas removed from the centre will be
richer in U235 by between 1.05 and 1.3 times. An
enrichment plant will have a sequence of stages, called
an enrichment cascade, and will have several hundred
cascades running at the same time.

Inside a nuclear power station

In many ways a nuclear power station is similar to a **fossil fuel** power station. A source of fuel (coal, gas or oil in a fossil fuel station) is used to provide energy to heat water to produce high-energy steam. The steam is used to spin a **turbine** which is used to generate electricity.

A worker changes fuel rods in a nuclear power station in Switzerland.

The reactor core

The heart of a nuclear power station is the **reactor** core. This is where the nuclear fuel is kept and where it undergoes **fission** to produce energy. The fuel is in the form of **fuel rods**. These are pellets or rods of fuel held in thin-walled metal containers, called **cladding**. A fuel element is made up of a number of fuel rods bundled together with spaces between them through which **coolants** can flow. There will be 200 or more fuel elements in a typical reactor. A fuel element produces energy for three to six years before it has to be replaced.

Coolants

Gas or liquid coolant passes through the reactor core and carries the heat away to the steam generators. The coolant comes into contact only with the cladding and not with the nuclear fuel. A coolant must not react with the cladding, which is extremely hot. It must not absorb too many **neutrons** because this would slow down the **chain reactions**. The coolant should also be inexpensive. Most reactors use carbon dioxide and helium gases or water as coolants.

The heated coolant is pumped to the steam generators. If water is used it may be allowed to boil, so producing steam directly. This is called a direct steam cycle. Otherwise, it may be used to heat a separate water supply – an indirect steam cycle. The coolant is pumped back to the reactor after the steam has been generated.

Moderators

A **moderator** surrounds the fuel rods and slows down neutrons so that they have a greater chance of striking nuclei. It is usually a material such as graphite.

Pressure vessels and shielding

The coolant in a nuclear reactor is kept under pressure, and for this reason the reactor core is surrounded by a pressure vessel. It is very important that the people working in a nuclear power plant are shielded from harmful **radiation**. The pressure vessel gives some protection but there is an additional shield called the biological shield, or simply 'the shield'. The shield has to be thick enough to protect the workers from neutrons and **gamma radiation** at all times. Concrete is a very good shielding material and a thickness of about two to three metres usually surrounds a reactor.

Control and containment

Several steps are taken to make sure that **radioactive** materials stay inside the nuclear **reactor**. The **cladding** should keep the **fission** products in the **fuel rods**, but if they do escape they will enter the **coolant**. The coolant flows in a closed loop around the reactor, meaning that it does not come into contact with anything else. However, if there is a leak in the coolant circuit then **radioactivity** will escape. But even then, there is an extra barrier to stop radioactivity spreading to the outside world. The barrier is the reactor building itself.

Reactor control

The **chain reactions** in a nuclear reactor can be controlled by using **control rods**. Boron, a non-metallic **element** is often used. These rods can be moved in and out of the reactor as necessary. They prevent **neutrons** from flying around. The fewer neutrons there are flying around, the fewer chain reactions will take place. The reactor can be shut down by adding the control rods. The reactor can be started up again by simply removing the rods.

Nuclear reactor control rods are inserted into the reactor core to slow down the chain reactions.

A reactor may have fifty or more control rods spread throughout the core. The operators of the power station can control the output of the reactor by adjusting the positions of the rods. By moving them in and out they can make the reactor produce more or less energy.

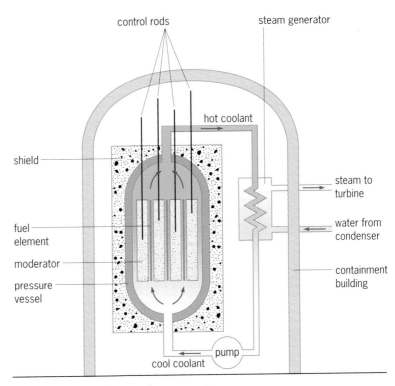

Cross-section of a reactor.

Shutdown rods

As well as the control rods, a reactor is also equipped with shutdown rods. These are absorbers that are kept out of the core when the reactor is running or in the core when the reactor has been shut down. The shutdown rods are controlled independently of the control rods. They are used to stop the chain reactions in an emergency.

Fission product heating

Even when the reactor has been shut down it will still go on producing heat. The chain reactions can be stopped by using control rods but there is no way of stopping the natural breakdown of the radioactive materials. This heat is called fission product heating. If steps are not taken to remove this heat the fuel may melt. Therefore, it is essential that the reactor core is cooled all the time, even when it is not producing energy. Emergency core cooling systems can be used if the main cooling system fails.

Reactor systems

Nuclear power stations around the world have different designs. Here we shall look at the more common types.

Advanced gas-cooled reactors (AGRs)

Advanced gas-cooled **reactors** supply over half of the electricity produced by nuclear reactors in Britain. The AGR followed the Magnox reactors, the first to be built in Britain, in the 1960s. Magnox reactors produced low temperature steam and were inefficient. In May 2000 it was confirmed that all of Britain's Magnox reactors were to be shut down.

AGRs use enriched uranium dioxide as their fuel. As the name suggests, AGRs use gas (carbon dioxide) as their **coolant**. Cooling channels are cut into blocks of graphite. The fuel is placed in these channels and coolant flows around them.

Dismantling one of Britain's out-dated Magnox reactors is a lengthy and hazardous process.

The pressure vessel surrounding the core is made of concrete four to six metres thick, with a thin lining of stainless steel to stop the coolant gas from escaping. After heating, the coolant gas is pumped to the steam generators. Once the steam has been generated, the coolant is sent back to the reactor core for use again. The steam drives a steam **turbine** to produce electricity. An AGR produces a continuous output of around 600 megawatts of electricity.

Pressurized water reactors (PWRs)

Pressurized water reactors are the most common type of reactor in the world. They use normal water as both their coolant and their **moderator**. The core of a PWR reactor is smaller than that of an AGR. Some of the **fuel rods** are left out to make room for the **control rods** and shutdown rods, which move up and down within the fuel elements. The whole core in enclosed by a 20-centimetre-thick steel pressure vessel. PWRs produce around 1000 megawatts of electricity.

The PWR has no cooling channels and the fuel elements are packed closely together. So the coolant passes up through the core between the fuel rods and is then pumped to a steam generator. After off-loading its heat, the coolant is pumped back to the reactor to be used again.

A pressurizer keeps a constant coolant pressure going. There is a pressure release valve in case the pressure gets too high. This is an essential part of the power station – if it goes wrong it can be disastrous. If the cooling system burst open the high pressure water inside would turn to steam instantly. This would massively increase the pressure inside the building and could blast open the walls.

A PWR nuclear power station in California, USA.

Fast breeders, fast movers

Fast breeder **reactors** are used to produce new **fissile** material in the form of plutonium. A breeder reactor can produce as much fuel as it uses. This is possible because when U238 absorbs a **neutron** in the reactor, it is changed into plutonium 239, a fissile material that can itself be used as nuclear fuel.

A typical breeder reactor has an inner core made up of lots of stainless-steel tubes filled with a mixture of uranium **oxide** and plutonium oxide. This is surrounded by an outer blanket of tubes of uranium oxide. This captures neutrons that escape from the core and the uranium is converted into plutonium. Heat is removed from the core by a liquid **coolant** and used to produce steam, which powers a **turbine** that drives a generator.

The core of a fast breeder reactor is small as it has no **moderator**. It produces a great deal of heat. Liquid sodium is often used as a coolant. The **heat energy** produced by the reactor core is so high that the fuel would melt in seconds if the coolant stopped flowing for any reason. For extra protection, the whole core is placed in a pool of liquid sodium into which heat can pass if the coolant system fails.

The reactor room at Beloyarskay a fast breeder in Russia.

An experimental fast breeder reactor site in the United States.

Superphénix, super failure?

The world's first commercial fast breeder was the Superphénix, built in France. It began to produce electricity in 1986 but it has had to be shutdown many time since. In the United States environmental concerns and the fear of plutonium falling into the hands of terrorists have stopped the development of breeder reactors. Britain shut down its first and only breeder reactor in 1994. Japan has continued its breeder development program but not without problems. In December 1995 a coolant pipe burst in Japan's prototype breeder, Monju, and an estimated 2 to 5 tonnes of liquid sodium was spilled, and then caught fire.

Nuclear energy on the move

The United States Navy soon saw how important an energy source nuclear power could be. It began a program to develop a naval reactor in the late 1940s. In 1954 the first nuclear submarine, the *Nautilus*, was launched. Today many of the world's navies use nuclear-powered submarines that can spend long periods underwater.

Spent fuel and reprocessing

Nuclear fuel lasts about six years in a **reactor**. After it is removed, it is called spent fuel. This spent fuel consists of uranium, plutonium and a variety of **fission** products. It is extremely hazardous. It is about 100 million times more **radioactive** than fresh fuel because all the fission products are themselves radioactive. Spent fuel can either be stored or it can be reprocessed.

Reprocessing

After its removal from the reactor, spent fuel is stored in water ponds 10 metres deep for a year or so to allow some of the shorter-lived fission products to **decay**. This makes it slightly less hazardous for the workers who will handle it later. The water also cools the fuel.

The spent fuel is then transported in special flasks to a reprocessing plant. In a test a transport flask was placed in front of a 140-tonne locomotive travelling at 160 kilometres per hour. After the collision the flask was still intact!

A flask for transporting spent nuclear fuel sits on a railway carriage.

The first stage in reprocessing is to chop up the **fuel rods** and dissolve them in nitric acid. This releases gaseous fission products, some of which have to be collected and disposed of. These, plus the fuel **cladding**, become another waste problem.

The next stage is to separate the uranium and plutonium from the fission products. The fission products then have to be stored as high-level waste. The uranium and plutonium are separated from each other. Nearly all of this material is stored. They could be used for reactor fuel at some point in the future if uranium became scarce.

Reprocessing and nuclear weapons

Reprocessing is the link between nuclear reactors and nuclear weapons because it provides the plutonium to make weapons. The United States banned commercial fuel reprocessing in the 1970s.

Storage cylinders containing uranium 238.

Dealing with nuclear waste

Radioactive waste is a big problem for the nuclear industry. Low-level nuclear waste includes **contaminated** clothing, packing material and fittings from nuclear **reactors**. Middle-level wastes include fuel **cladding** and wastes from fuel reprocessing. These require more careful storage than low-level wastes.

Low-level nuclear wastes have been placed in concrete-lined trenches and covered with soil at waste sites. Controversially, liquid low-level wastes have simply been pumped into the sea. This caused particular outrage when wastes from the Sellafield reprocessing plant in Cumbria were pumped into the Irish Sea.

High-level waste disposal

High-level waste includes spent **fuel rods** and **fission** products such as plutonium. Spent fuel produces so much heat that it has to be cooled for decades.

Disposal of wastes is not the same as storage. Stored wastes are kept safe and accessible for possible future treatment or use. Disposal means that the wastes are put safely out of reach.

Spent nuclear fuel is encased in glass in a reprocessing plant.

First the waste is encased in a special strong glass. Next, the waste is encased in 25-centimetre-thick stainless-steel containers. These containers can then be placed in underground shafts up to 1000 metres deep. The tunnels are then filled with materials that prevent water from getting at the containers. The tunnel walls may also be lined with concrete. The final barrier is the hundreds of metres of rock between the waste and the surface.

Yucca Mountain, Nevada, where the US government plans to build a nuclear waste depository.

The nuclear industry is still storing rather than disposing of wastes. The US Department of Energy had to begin accepting spent nuclear fuel for disposal in 1998, but it will be at least 2010 before its fuel burial site in Yucca Mountain, Nevada, is ready.

How long to store?

It is very difficult to say how quickly radioactive wastes **decay**. There will be a range of different radioactive **isotopes** in the waste, each with a different **half-life**

Storing the wastes for ten years will reduce **radioactivity** significantly and there is a rapid fall between 100 and 1000 years after which the isotopes decay slowly. Spent fuel has to be kept cooled for decades. It must also be kept out of contact with the rest of the environment for hundreds of years at the very least.

Disposal dilemma

A major problem in disposing of nuclear waste lies in finding a suitable site. No matter how much the industry or government might say that the waste is safely locked away, people still won't want it buried near them.

A train-load of nuclear waste on its way to a disposal site passes the village of Seascale in Cumbria.

Can we be certain?

Nuclear waste has to be kept isolated for a thousand years at the very least but no one can ever say with absolute certainty that a waste disposal site will remain secure over all this time. This makes choosing waste sites a very difficult task. For a small country such as Britain there may be no acceptable sites for high-level waste disposal. Many people believe that, at present, we have as yet no real solution to the problem of nuclear waste. It seems that, for the foreseeable future, high-level waste will have to be disposed of near the surface.

A wider problem

Of course, nuclear waste disposal is by no means the only disposal problem we have to face. We are rapidly running out of places for new landfill sites for the millions of tonnes of household and industrial waste we create. Many people believe that the haphazard 'disposal' of carbon dioxide waste from **fossil fuel** power stations and other sources straight into the atmosphere is leading to global climate changes. Better management of hazardous wastes of all kinds is an issue that has to be faced.

To reprocess or not to reprocess?

An advantage of reprocessing is that is concentrates the dangerous high-level waste into a small volume. A major disadvantage is in having stockpiles of plutonium to deal with. For many, the hazards involved are a strong argument against reprocessing and for the long-term storage of spent fuel.

Waste production

At each stage in the reprocessing, wastes are produced. From the reprocessing of four cubic metres of spent fuel from a typical PWR **reactor**, about 650 cubic metres of waste are produced. In contrast, a coal-fired power station with a similar power output leaves about 300,000 cubic metres of ash to be disposed of.

Spent nuclear fuel from Japan arrives in Britain for reprocessing.

Radiation and life

Radiation – silent, invisible, odourless and potentially deadly – is something that we fear. Our senses give us no warning of radiation being near and this, perhaps, also makes it seem frightening. So what does radiation actually do to living things?

Particle radiation

Radiation can be divided into two groups. First, electromagnetic radiation, which includes radio waves, visible light, X-rays and **gamma rays**. Second, particle radiation, such as the **neutrons**, **alpha particles** and **beta particles**, given off by **radioactive decay**.

When alpha or beta particles pass through matter they can disrupt the bonds that hold **atoms** together in **molecules**. Bonds can be broken and new ones may be formed.

A Geiger counter is used to detect radioactivity.

This process is called ionization and radiation that does this is called **ionizing radiation**.

If these chemical changes take place in a living organism they can bring about biological changes that could be harmful. The amount of energy needed to cause damage to a living thing is tiny. (For example, the amount of ionizing radiation needed to kill an adult human is equivalent to the energy needed to raise the body temperature by only 0.0025°Celsius.)

The effect on cells

Radiation can damage any part of a living **cell**. Damage to the cell **nucleus** tends to be the most serious because this is where the cell's DNA is found. DNA is rather like a chemical codebook carrying the instructions the cell needs to work properly. If the cell's DNA is damaged it may no longer be able to divide. This can have terrible effects, for example, on cells lining the intestines. Here, cell division takes place continually as new surface cells grow to protect cells underneath.

Another possibility is that the damaged cell divides uncontrollably. This can result in cancer. Sometimes the damage done to the DNA may be passed on to the person's children. This damage could result in miscarriage, stillbirth or in a baby being born with major life-threatening defects.

Cells do have repair mechanisms. However, the repair mechanisms can fail if there is a very large dose of radiation, or several doses separated by short periods of time.

Workers have to wear special protective radiation suits to carry out hazardous decontamination duties.

Dosage and damage

Workers in a nuclear power plant will wear 'dosimeters' like this to monitor exposure to any radiation.

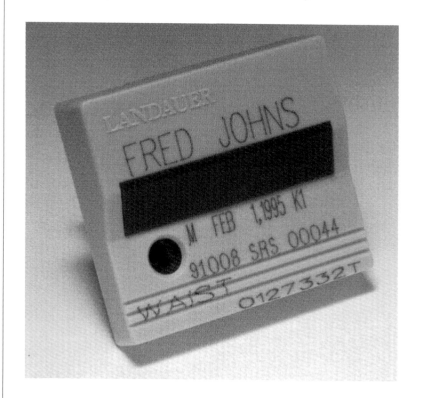

The damage done to living organisms depends on the type of **radiation**. **Alpha particles** are emitted by **elements** such as uranium and plutonium. The range of an alpha particle is very short – it will not get through the outer skin layers – and it gives up its energy rapidly. Damage is mainly in a few **cells** only but it is difficult to repair. Alpha radiation is a serious hazard if it gets inside the body, for example if uranium mineworkers breathe in **radioactive** dust particles.

Beta particles have a greater range than alpha particles and can go deeper into the body. The damage they cause is spread over a greater distance but can be more easily repaired.

Gamma radiation is highly penetrating. Gamma rays are dangerous because they can penetrate deep into the body tissues, reaching right into the bone marrow where our blood cells are made.

Safe levels?

Deciding on a safe level of exposure to any dangerous substance, not just radioactive, is very difficult. By 'safe' do we mean no risk at all? This is just not possible in the real world so we have to decide instead what level of risk we are prepared to accept. Having done that (no easy task!), the next thing is to decide what level of radiation exposure matches the risk we are prepared to take. Once again, this is not easy. At lower levels of exposure the best we can do is to say that there is a chance that the exposure could lead to a fatal cancer. We can also say that this risk increases with increasing exposure. What we cannot do is to state absolutely that the effect will be the same in every person exposed to a certain level of radiation.

Setting the limits

The International Commission on Radiological Protection has set recommendations on radiation dose limits. Nothing involving exposure to radiation should be done unless it is for the overall benefit of the population. Those who oppose reprocessing of nuclear waste, for example, claim it produces no benefit and so radiation exposure from reprocessing cannot be justified.

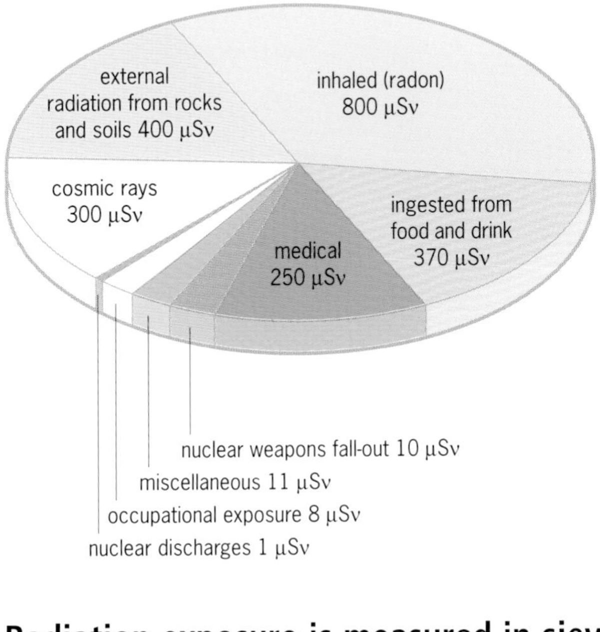

external radiation from rocks and soils 400 µSv

inhaled (radon) 800 µSv

cosmic rays 300 µSv

ingested from food and drink 370 µSv

medical 250 µSv

nuclear weapons fall-out 10 µSv
miscellaneous 11 µSv
occupational exposure 8 µSv
nuclear discharges 1 µSv

Radiation exposure is measured in sieverts (Sv). Humans can absorb 0.25 Sv without ill effects, 1.5 Sv can produce radiation sickness; 8 Sv is fatal. This chart shows exposure for the average person from various sources in millionths (µ) of Sv.

Reactor accidents

The biggest danger from nuclear power comes from the damaging effects of exposure to **radioactive** materials. So far major accidents at **reactors** have been very rare events. But they have happened – and could happen again.

Windscale

In October 1957 a standard procedure went wrong in the reactor at Windscale, Cumbria. So far this has been the most serious accident at a reactor in Britain. The temperature rose in the reactor and both the graphite **moderator** and the uranium fuel caught fire. Radioactive materials escaped into the atmosphere. As a result, milk from 500 square kilometres around the site had to be destroyed so that radioactive material did not get into human food. The workers and many people living nearby received far greater doses of radiation than are allowed. A report issued by the National Radiological Protection Board in 1982 suggested that 32 more cancer deaths than normal happened as a result of the **contamination**.

The nuclear power station at Three Mile Island, Pennsylvania.

Three Mile Island

On 28 March 1979, a pump circulating cooling water in one of two PWRs at Three Mile Island, Harrisburg, Pennsylvania, stopped operating. The **coolant** immediately began to heat up dangerously but the automatic emergency cooling systems kicked in and safely shut down the reactor.

However the operators mistakenly thought there was too much water in the core, so they turned the emergency cooling system off. The water in the primary cooling circuit started to boil and the **cladding** on the **fuel rods** began to melt. By the time cooling was fully working again a third of the fuel had melted and the containment building was **contaminated**. The reactor was never used again.

Expecting the unexpected

Accidents in nuclear power stations can have such catastrophic results it is essential that they are dealt with efficiently. One way of doing this is to use reactor simulators. A computer simulates the way a reactor works under different circumstances, giving the operator the chance to learn how to deal with a variety of events.

Workers at Three Mile Island practise retrieving items from a model of the damaged reactor.

Chernobyl and beyond

The worst nuclear accident to happen so far was at a **reactor** in Chernobyl, near the town of Pripyat in the former Soviet Union (now in the Ukraine), on 26 April 1986. The Chernobyl reactor had been in operation since 1984 and was one of the Soviet Union's most successful nuclear power stations.

As part of a safety study, a test was run to find out how long the electricity generators would continue to work if the steam supply to the **turbine** was cut off. During the test the power level fell uncontrollably. The reactor should have shutdown automatically, but the operators prevented this. Despite the problems, they decided to go ahead with the test and shut off the steam supply to the turbines.

Out of control

At this point only seven **control rods** were in the core, even though the operating instructions required a minimum of thirty. The reactor began to run out of control and the control rods could not be inserted quickly enough to regain control. Within three to four seconds the power rose to a hundred times its maximum level. A chemical explosion followed, as the molten fuel reacted with the cooling water

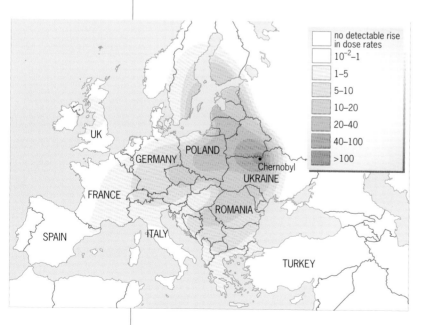

no detectable rise in dose rates
10^{-2}–1
1–5
5–10
10–20
20–40
40–100
>100

How radiation levels rose across Europe after the Chernobyl disaster.

and blasted the 2000-tonne reactor cap off. **Fission** products from the core were lifted high into the atmosphere and streamed out for ten days before the fire was brought under control.

Russia today

Sosnovy-Bor, a suburb of St Petersburg, has a digital Geiger counter on the town hall displaying local **radiation** levels in large red letters. The town's only industry is the Leningrad Nuclear Power Plant, a Chernobyl-type power station. If Chernobyl's explosion had happened here, many of the four million people of St Petersburg would have received a massive dose of radiation.

The massive damage caused by the explosion at Chernobyl is clearly shown.

The US Department of Energy has a secret list of the world's seven most dangerous reactors – all are in the former Soviet Union. 'Many Soviet-designed reactors ... pose significant safety risks,' the agency said in a 1995 report, and 'these reactors continue to experience serious incidents ...'

Could it happen again?

Asked if he thought another Chernobyl could happen, a spokesman for the International Atomic Energy Agency said, 'I don't think so. Safety has improved throughout the world. But there are no guarantees. And there's absolutely no reason for complacency. We have to do our best and cross our fingers.' Does that sound reassuring?

Nuclear future

In the 1980s orders for new nuclear **reactor** constructions and for stations to start up ranged from 20 to 40 per year. By 1997 there were just two new orders, and five start-ups worldwide. It is concern about money, not **radiation** bringing about the end of the nuclear power industry. Nuclear power plants need increasingly expensive maintenance as they get older. It won't be easy to shut the reactors down. Around 16 per cent of the world's power now comes from nuclear plants, so alternatives will have to be found.

The end of the nuclear dream?

Britain became the first European country to take a reactor out of operation, when it was decided in 1999 to close down the Dounreay power station near Thurso on Scotland's northern coast. The cleanup and shutdown process could take up to a hundred years and cost £500 million. The decision was made after mysterious **radioactive** particles were found on local beaches. The sand-like particles are radioactive enough to blister someone who sits on them. Officials say they don't know how they escaped.

Nuclear fusion

Some people see nuclear **fusion** as the way forward. Nuclear fusion is the opposite of nuclear **fission**. It happens when the **nuclei** of two lighter **atoms** combine to form a heavier one, rather than a heavy nucleus splitting apart. The resulting atom has a smaller mass than the original ones, because some of the mass has been transformed into energy. This is what happens in an atomic bomb explosion. Gram for gram, fusion produces eight times more energy than the fission of uranium, and over a million times more than could be obtained by burning the same weight of **fossil fuels**.

Fusion is not only desirable because it is such a wonderful energy source, but also because the fuels used are fairly plentiful. Also, the product from the reaction is just unreactive helium gas, rather than polluting gases and radioactive waste.

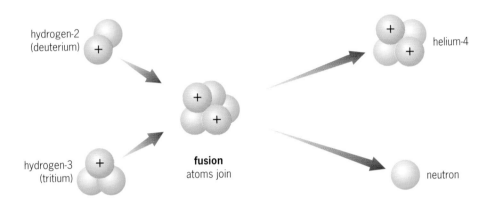

hydrogen-2 (deuterium)

hydrogen-3 (tritium)

fusion atoms join

helium-4

neutron

Two **isotopes** of hydrogen undergo fusion to become helium plus a **neutron**.

Research on controlled fusion energy is taking place in many countries, particularly the United States, Japan and the European Union. However, in experiments so far, the energy obtained in the laboratory has hardly been more than the energy put in to run the tests. Fusion reactions are difficult to achieve because the nuclei have to be made to collide at very high speeds and need heating to a temperature of 100 million°Celsius or more.

A nuclear fusion test reactor at Princeton University in the United States.

The extremely high cost of fusion research, and the uncertainty of ever making money out of it makes most businesses and governments very unwilling to finance its development.

Nuclear power – nuclear weapons

The discovery that vast amounts of energy could be released by splitting the atom was an exciting one. It promised a new source of power for society. However it was not the desire to benefit society by introducing a new energy source that drove people to harness atomic power. Instead, it was to produce a bomb. The successful detonation of the first atomic bomb at Los Alamos, New Mexico, in the United States on 16 July 1945 marked a new era. In the decades to come the threat of nuclear destruction would hang over the Earth.

Building a bomb

Atomic or nuclear bombs fall into two types – **fission** weapons and **fusion** weapons. Fission weapon contains pure, or nearly pure, plutonium 239 or uranium enriched to over 90 per cent U235. Around the outside of the bomb is a layer of ordinary explosives. When these explosives are triggered the **fissile** material is compressed. This heats it to the point where fission starts to happen, causing a runaway **chain reaction** and a massive explosion within millionths of a second.

An American airman surveys the devastation caused by the atomic bomb dropped on Hiroshima.

A fusion weapon uses the power of a fission bomb to provide the energy needed to heat up and compress hydrogen **isotopes** so they fuse together, releasing devastating amounts of energy. Because fusion weapons use hydrogen, they are often called hydrogen bombs.

Bomb energy

The bomb dropped on Nagasaki in World War II released the equivalent of 20,000 tonnes of TNT (a common explosive).

Weapons production

If a country wants to build nuclear weapons it needs a supply of fissile material. This means having either a uranium enrichment facility or a nuclear **reactor** to produce plutonium and a reprocessing plant to extract it. The average amount of plutonium needed to make a weapon is 10 kilograms. If a country possesses either a uranium enrichment facility or a reprocessing plant then it could make nuclear weapons.

Tension grew between India and Pakistan in 1998 when India ran five underground nuclear weapons tests near the Pakistan border.

Nuclear countries

Some countries have nuclear power, but do not (so far as we know) have nuclear weapons. These include Canada, Japan, Sweden and the Netherlands.

International Nuclear Event Scale

The International Nuclear Event Scale (INES) was designed to tell the public about the safety issues of reported events at nuclear plants. There are seven levels, with level 7 the most dangerous.

7 Major accident   External release of a large fraction of the **radioactive** material in a large facility resulting in the possibility of acute health effects; delayed health effects over a wide area, possibly involving more than one country; long-term environmental consequences. Example: Chernobyl, USSR (now Ukraine), 1986.

6 Serious accident   External release of radioactive material likely to result in full implementation of countermeasures covered by local emergency plans to limit serious health effects. Example: Kyshtym Reprocessing Plant, USSR (now Russia), 1957.

5 Accident with off site risk   External release of radioactive material likely to result in partial implementation of countermeasures covered by emergency plans. Severe damage to the nuclear facility, such as a major criticality accident or a major fire or explosion releasing large quantities of **radioactivity** within the installation. Examples: Windscale Pile, UK, 1957; Three Mile Island, USA, 1979.

4 Accident without significant off-site risk
External release of radioactivity resulting in little need for off-site protective actions except possibly for local food control. Significant damage to the nuclear facility, such as damage to a nuclear plant leading to major on-site recovery problems such as partial core melt in a power **reactor**. Irradiation of one or more workers resulting in an overexposure where a high probability of early death occurs. Examples: Windscale Reprocessing Plant, UK, 1973; Saint-Laurent NPP, France, 1980; Buenos Aires Critical Assembly, Argentina, 1983.

3 Serious incident   External release of radioactivity above authorized limits, resulting in doses to workers sufficient to cause acute health effects. Example: Vandellos NPP, Spain, 1989.

2 Incident   Incidents with significant failure in safety provisions or an event resulting in a dose to a worker exceeding a statutory annual dose limit and/or an event that leads to the presence of significant quantities of radioactivity in the installation.

1 Anomaly   Event occurring beyond authorized limits due to equipment failure, human error or procedural inadequacies.

Chronology

1896 French physicist Antoine Henri Becquerel discovers radioactivity

1905 Albert Einstein shows that **mass** and energy can be converted from one to the other

1919 New Zealand physicist Ernest Rutherford splits the **atom**, by bombarding a nitrogen **nucleus** with **alpha particles**

1939 Otto Hahn, Fritz Strassmann, and Lise Meitner announce the discovery of nuclear **fission**

1942 Enrico Fermi builds the first nuclear reactor, in a squash court at the University of Chicago, USA

1945 The first atom bomb is detonated at Los Alamos, New Mexico

1951 The Experimental Breeder Reactor, Idaho, USA, produces the first electricity to be generated by **nuclear energy**

1956 The world's first commercial nuclear power station, Calder Hall, comes into operation in the UK

1957 Release of **radiation** from Windscale (now Sellafield) nuclear power station, Cumbria, England. In Kyshtym, USSR, escape of plutonium waste caused an unknown number of casualties. On maps produced the following year 30 small communities had been deleted.

1979 Nuclear reactor accident at Three Mile Island, Pennsylvania, USA

1986 Explosion in a reactor at Chernobyl results in clouds of radioactive material spreading as far as Sweden

1991 The first controlled production of nuclear **fusion** energy is achieved at Joint European Torus (JET), Culham, Oxfordshire, England

1995 Sizewell B, the UK's first pressurized water nuclear reactor and the most advanced nuclear power station in the world, begins operating in Suffolk, England

1997 English physicists at JET produce a record 12 megawatts of nuclear fusion power

1999 Japan's worst-ever nuclear accident results in 49 people, mostly plant workers, being exposed to potentially harmful levels of radiation

Glossary

alpha particle   positively charged, high energy particle consisting of two protons and two neutrons emitted from the nucleus of a radioactive atom. Releasing an alpha particle transforms one element into another.

atomic number   number of protons in the nucleus of an atom. Every element has a different atomic number.

atoms   smallest units of matter that can take part in a chemical reaction, and the smallest parts of an element that can exist

beta particle   electron ejected at high speed from the nucleus of a radioactive atom. They are created when a neutron changes into a proton, an electron as it does so.

boron   used in the making of control rods for reactors because of its ability to absorb neutrons

cells   smallest units of life capable of independent existence

chain reaction   fission reaction in which neutrons released by the splitting of atomic nuclei strike other nuclei causing them to split and release more neutrons, which cause still more nuclei to split, and so on

chemical energy   energy held in the bonds that hold atoms together in molecules. Chemical energy is released during a chemical reaction

cladding   metal covering around a rod or pellet of fissile material

compound   chemical substance made up of two or more atoms of different elements bonded together

contaminate   to make impure by adding unwanted or undesirable substances

control rod   rod of material which slows a nuclear reaction by absorbing neutrons

coolant   fluid used to remove heat from reactor core and transfer it to the generators

decay   the breaking up of the nuclei of radioactive elements

diffuse   to mingle with another substance through the movement of particles

electron   one of the subatomic particles that make up an atom. Electrons have a negative electric charge and orbit around the central nucleus of the atom.

element   substance that cannot be split into a simpler substance by means of a chemical reaction

fissile   materials that will break apart and release energy when struck by a neutron

fission   splitting of a large atomic nucleus into two or more fragments with the release of energy

fossil fuels   fuels produced through the action of heat and pressure on the fossil remains of plants and animals that lived millions of years ago. The fossil fuels are coal, petroleum and natural gas.

fuel rod   rod or pellet of fissile material, usually uranium, together with its protective cladding, used to power a nuclear reactor

fusion   process by which two small atomic nuclei combine to produce a single larger nucleus with the release of a great deal of energy

gamma radiation (rays)   high energy, short wavelength radiation released from a radioactive atom

half-life   time it takes for half of a quantity of a radioactive substance to decay. Half-lives can vary from billionths of a second to billions of years.

heat energy   energy to do with the motion of atoms

ionizing radiation   radiation that alters the bonds in an atom by knocking electrons off the atom

isotopes   atoms that have the same number of protons (and are therefore the same chemical element) but which have different numbers of neutrons and so have different atomic masses

kinetic energy   the energy of movement

mass   the amount of matter in an object

meltdown   where the reactor core melts as a result of the fuel overheating

moderator   material used in a nuclear reactor to reduce the speed of high-energy neutrons and so control the rate at which energy is produced

molecule   two or more atoms joined together by chemical bonds

neutron   one of the subatomic particles that make up an atom. Neutrons have no electric charge and are found in the central nucleus of the atom.

nuclear energy   (also called atomic energy) energy in the nucleus of an atom released when a large nucleus breaks down into two smaller nuclei (fission) or when two small nuclei combine to form a larger nucleus (fusion)

nucleus   central part of an atom, made up of protons and neutrons and containing nearly all of the atom's mass

ore   raw material from which a substance is purified

oxide   compound (blend) that contains oxygen

proton   one of the subatomic particles that make up an atom. Protons have a positive electric charge and are found in the central nucleus.

radiation   energy given off in the form of fast-moving particles or electromagnetic waves as a result of the decay of an atomic nucleus

radioactive   describes a substance that gives off radiation

radioactivity   the release of radiation from a substance in the forms of alpha and beta particles and gamma rays

reactor   structure in which radioactive material is made to breakdown in a controlled way, releasing energy that can be put to use

turbine   engine in which a fluid is used to spin a shaft by pushing on angled blades like those on a fan

Index

Titles in the *Energy for life* series include:

Hardback   0 431 14642 X

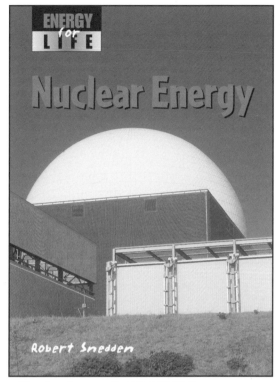

Hardback   0 431 14640 3

Hardback   0 431 14644 6

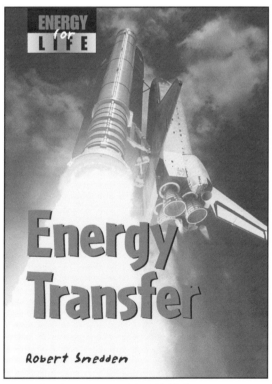

Hardback   0 431 14646 2

Find out about the other titles in this series on our website www.heinemann.co.uk/library